the
practice
of the
presence
of god

THE
PRACTICE
OF THE
PRESENCE
OF GOD

BROTHER LAWRENCE OF THE
RESURRECTION

Translated by
DONALD ATTWATER

Introduction by
DOROTHY DAY

TEMPLEGATE
SPRINGFIELD, ILLINOIS

CONTENTS

SPIRITUAL MAXIMS

Some Reflections on Brother Lawrence and the Practice of the Presence of God

Dorothy Day

This book, made up of a few conversations, a few letters, has come down to us through the centuries, and is too little known. It is a classic, and carries a message, points a way. It tells of a spirituality which is within the reach of all. Most men and women have to work for a living. A philosopher once said "Do what you are doing "—that is, pay attention to what you are doing. Brother Lawrence obviously had no books in his kitchen, to study ways of finding God. He had to find his way, obviously by prayer.

But how to pray? St. Teresa of Avila wrote many books on prayer, St. John of the Cross too, and books have been written about their books, further expounding the meaning of prayer. St. Paul told us all to search the scriptures and to pray without ceasing.

Both commands must have presented difficulties to an ex-soldier, who spent his life in a kitchen or in the market place finding the bread and wine, meat and vegetables for a community. Certainly there was little time for the delightful occupation of **reading** about prayer.

I am sure the disciples of Jesus did little reading, fishermen as they were, many of them. They asked him, "How shall we pray?"

He gave them the Lord's prayer. He, God-man that he was, told them no other prayer.

Pope John XXIII, a peasant priest writing to his peasant family, had this commentary:

"I repeat: to know how to say the Our Father and to know how to put it into practice, this is the perfection of the Christian Life." (Letters to His Family, p. 449)

"In the Lord's prayer we have a summary of the entire Gospel," Tertullian wrote.

Entire books have been written about the Lord's Prayer but there is no mention of books in Brother Lawrence's reported conversations and letters. His serenity, his simplicity is that of the prayer Jesus Christ taught us. "Ask and you shall receive. Seek and you shall find." Jesus taught us what to ask for and, as Pascal commented, "You would not seek Him, if you had not already found Him."

*   *   *

Brother Lawrence's times were no different from ours. St. Teresa of Avila, who lived in the time of the Inquisition, wrote, "All times are dangerous times." Just as St. Paul called upon us to be other Christs, Lawrence was another Christ, who lived in the presence of the Father at all times.

He grew up like other children and young men, and went through a conversion of heart at the age of sixteen. He had one of those striking experiences that I think we all have, whether we live in the country or in the city. "One winter day he noticed a tree stripped of its leaves and reflected that before long

9

leaves would appear anew, then flowers and then the fruit, and that this consideration gave him so striking an idea of the Providence and might of God that it had never since been effaced from his soul;... and kindled in him so great a love for God that he was not able to say if it had at all increased during the forty-odd years which had since passed."

We have to leap into faith through the senses—from the natural to the supernatural—and I was drawn to the Church in my youth because it appealed to the senses. The music speaking to the ear, the incense to the sense of smell, the appeal of color to the eye, stained glass, ikons and statues, the bread and wine to the taste, the touch of rich vestments and altar linens, the touch of holy water, oils, the sign of the cross, the beating of the breast.

When my own mother was dying, she asked me quietly and soberly, "What about a future life?" I could only point to the flowers which surrounded her. It was in the fall and there were giant chrysanthemums filling the tables in her room. It was like a promise from God, and God keeps his promises. I pointed to the trees outside, stripped of their leaves, looking dead to the eye from that distance, but there had recently been a blaze of glory in the color of the maples. Another sign of a promise. Later she said, "I can only pray the Our Father and the Creed. Is that enough?" And when I thought of the books which would fill libraries which had been written on every phrase contained in the Our Father, it comforted my heart to know that she was practicing the presence of God this way.

*   *   *

The Practice of the Presence of God consists of conversations, letters, and maxims on how we should live, with the idea of cultivating this sense of the presence of God in the soul, and indeed in the world about us.

The very word "sense" might seem to throw us off, because the whole book has to do with the spiritual life of man, not his sense life, and so can be brushed aside as non-sense. But we all have a desire for the

True, the Good and the Beautiful which is God. And we look around us today in a time of war and fear, of stockpiling for war, of greed, dishonesty, and ambition, and long for peace in our time, for that peace which passeth understanding, which we see only glimpses of, through a glass darkly.

(I cannot write and express myself without using the words and phrases of St. Paul, of scripture. We are told to "search the scripture" to find comfort and guidance. St. Therese of Lisieux who reminds me of Brother Lawrence in her practice of the "little way," said once that she could read fifty chapters of Isaiah and get nothing out of them and then suddenly the fifty-first flooded her soul with light. Which makes me think of the subconscious mind working away, and leaping on what it needs for sustenance, comfort, or understanding.)

When St. Paul says to pray always, to pray without ceasing, he is also talking about practicing the presence of God.

*   *   *

Dr. Robert Coles, a psychiatrist, in his book **A Spectacle unto the World,** wrote of the ordinariness of our work at the Catholic Worker and all of us engaged in it.

It is that flavor of ordinariness one gets from Brother Lawrence—not Saint Lawrence, or Blessed Lawrence, you will notice, but Brother Lawrence. If he had been called saint, Protestants might have ignored him in that day. As it was, they are the ones who have done much to popularize him. (Donald Attwater, in his preface, calls attention to the fact that he has been popular among the Huguenots in France and Protestants in England.)

All of us who love Brother Lawrence are brought closer together, just as those who love **The Imitation of Christ** are. **The Way of a Pilgrim** brings us closer to the Eastern Orthodox Churches. **Tales of the Hasidim** (whether told by Martin Buber, Elie Wiesel, or Abraham Heschel) brings us closer to Judaism. Coming closer to our brothers brings us closer to

God. **The Practice of the Presence of God** does this for us too.

*   *   *

Recently an old woman died in our midst, here at our House of Hospitality in New York. She was surrounded by many men and women she had known a long time; she had the best of care. We had a nurse living with us who could meet any emergency. But Catherine, the last few weeks of her life, often clutched at my hand as I passed her, and would plead with me, "There is a God, tell me there is a God! Tell me!"

I could only say, "Yes Catherine, there is a God. He is our Father and He loves us, you and me." When you say these things it is an act of faith. You feel your helplessness so you pray harder. You seem to know nothing, you can only hold her hand and make your affirmation. So much of our prayer is made up of these affirmations. "I praise Thee, O God, I bless Thee. What have I on earth but Thee and what do I desire in heaven besides Thee. I am saying this **for**

Catherine, **instead** of Catherine, because she is in 'the valley of the shadow.' "

But did I comfort her? A few days later a young girl said to me, "The word **Father** means nothing to me. It brings me no comfort. I had a drunken father who abused my mother and beat his children." We can do nothing by our words. So we are driven to prayer by our helplessness. God takes over.

*   *   *

Brother Lawrence evidently was not learned. He was a soldier, and was wounded "in a raid by the Swedes on the village of Rambervilliers in Lorraine where he was born." Perhaps the sight of the tree which brought about his conversion was during his convalescence. (The few words of his biography do not make that clear.) He went to work as a footman for a time, but his desire to live a religious life led him to join the Carmelite order. Donald Attwater, a gifted researcher in the lives of saints and near-saints, writes that Lawrence spent the last thirty years of his life in the kitchen of a monastery.

He lived and "had his being," as the saying goes, in that lowly place in the kitchen.

Brother Lawrence undoubtedly grew in grace because he performed manual labor. "Orare et Laborare" is the Benedictine creed—to pray and to work. The lowliness of his work and the fact that it was necessary work for the Order of the Universe and the Order of the Carmelite monastery to which he belonged: this brought him the peace of heart which has made him the influence he has been from that day to this.

We forget that Jesus was a carpenter before he was a teacher. Thirty years of his life were spent in a small village of Galilee. He grew up learning and practicing carpentry.

St. Paul worked at weaving even as he travelled the roads of the Roman Empire of his day. He earned his own living, he pointed out to his listeners. He did not hesitate to remind them that they had the obligation to support those who could not work, which might have meant the unemployed, the sick, the old and destitute. Fr. Vincent McNabb, the great English Dominican who used to preach in Hyde Park, London, talked of the dignity of work, and pointed out in a book of his, **Nazareth Or Social Chaos,** that Peter, the Rock, could go back to his nets after the death of his Lord, but that St. Matthew could not go back to his tax-gathering. That would be giving too much to Caesar in a wartime economy.

The desert Fathers, beginning with the great St. Anthony, practiced manual labor. St. Anthony's life was written by St. Athanasius who visited him when all the ancient world seemed to be turning Arian and denying the divinity of Christ. He found him weaving mats and baskets and living on sparse desert fare, as many of our own American Indians of Southwestern Arizona live off the desert around them to this day. The first monasteries began because of St. Anthony's example as a hermit.

Living today in a time of war, crying out Peace, Peace when there is no Peace, fearing age and death, pain and darkness, destitution and loneliness, people need to get back to the simplicity of Brother Lawrence.

Even the non-religious philosopher and scientist William James has extolled "the little way" in the realm of the natural world. He wrote in a letter to a friend. "As for me, my bed is made: I am against bigness and greatness in all their forms, and with the invisible molecular moral forces that work from individual to individual, stealing in through the crannies of the world like so many soft rootlets, or like the capillary oozing of water, and yet rending the hardest monuments of man's pride, if you give them time. The bigger the unit you deal with, the hollower, the more brutal, the more mendacious is the life displayed. So I am against all big organizations as such, national ones first and foremost; against all big successes and big results; and in favor of the external forces of truth which always work in the individual and immediately unsuccessful way, underdogs always, till history comes, after they are long dead, and puts them on the top."

Brother Lawrence did not have the tumultuous life of St. Teresa and St. John of the Cross (who lived in the century before him, in danger of the Inquisition, the latter imprisoned and beaten by his fellow monks, factions growing up in the church around them). Perhaps it was because he did not write, was not published. Yet, writes Attwater, "He was known and venerated by the whole of Paris. And not only by the crowd of nameless and poor Christians who, in all ages and places, have had such a genius for detecting sanctity, but also by the learned, the distinguished, and the noble, both clerical and lay."

* * *

We need this book today when we are overwhelmed by the vastness of today's problems. We need to return to the simplicity of a Brother Lawrence, whose "little way" makes our burdens light and rejoices the heart.

These days I can never look up at the sky and see the moon without thinking with wonder and awe that men have walked there. To conceive of such a thing

—to desire such an adventure, to be capable of overcoming all fear, all doubt, to have faith in man's ability to solve problems, and seek out the way to go about this great exploration—what dedication of mind and will!

"What is man that thou art mindful of him? Thou hast made him little less than the angels."

It keeps coming into my mind—how much man would be capable of if his soul were strong in the love of God, if he wanted God as much as he wanted to penetrate the power and glory of God's creation.

To know Him, to love Him and to serve Him—a personal God, who took on human flesh and became man and suffered and died for us.

To find the way, not to the moon but to God—this is man's real desire, because of his need for love, and God is love.

Brother Lawrence, who worked in the kitchen of a Carmelite monastery and died at the age of 80, found Him in "The Practice of the Presence of God."

EDITOR'S INTRODUCTION

I

The author of those writings and reported conversations generally known as **The Practice of the Presence of God** was born at Hérimesnil, in Lorraine, about the year 1611. His family name was Herman, he was christened Nicolas, and he was well brought up by his parents, who were religious folk. At the age of eighteen he became a soldier, but was wounded in a raid by the Swedes on the village of Rambervilliers, and he had to give up that profession. For some time he was a footman, but his naturally religious tendency, encouraged by the example of an uncle who was a Carmelite friar, impelled him towards the religious state.

Several times he attempted the life of a hermit, but was soon reduced to such a state of spiritual instability and uncertainty that he realized that he must submit himself to a rule. At last, after a further period of irresolution, he offered himself as a laybrother to the Discalced Carmelites of Paris; he was accepted, received the name of Lawrence-of-the-Resurrection, and was set to work in the kitchen.

The rest of his life may be found in his works. Abbé de Beaufort, vicar general of Cardinal de Noailles and chronicler of the **Conversations,** has written of him: "Nobody can paint the saints so well as they themselves . . . so nothing can bring this servant of God more clearly before you than his own words spoken in the simplicity of his heart." Br. Lawrence exemplified to a remarkable degree "the simplicity that is in Christ." He was very careful to avoid singularity, and "did not assume that melancholy pious air which only puts off ordinary people; he was not one of those persons who never unbend and who regard good manners as incompatible with holiness." De Beaufort tells us that he had a frank, open manner that invited confidence. "When he knew with whom he was dealing, he spoke freely, simply, to the point, and with good sense. Behind his rough appearance there was unusual wisdom, breadth of view and keenness."

The disposition of his heart and inner life are made plain in the following pages. "This disposition brought him to so great an unconcern about everything and to so complete a detachment, that it was near to the freedom of the Blessed. . . . Nothing could hold him to earth: his vision was not bounded by time: from long contemplation of Him who is eternal, his spirit had become as it were timeless."

He died as he had lived, finding in his last and painful illness the long-desired opportunity to suffer for God. He received the last sacraments, surrounded by his Carmelite brethren and, in his own words, "blessing God, praising God, worshipping God and loving Him with all my heart. That is our one business, brethren, to worship Him and love Him, without thought of anything else." He died at nine o'clock in the morning of Monday, February 12, 1691, being about eighty years of age.

Br. Lawrence's was a hidden life; his spirit was rapt in God, and his body for thirty years employed in the kitchen of a Carmelite monastery. Nevertheless, he was known to and revered by the whole of

Paris. And not only by the crowds of nameless and poor Christians who, in all ages and places, have had such a genius for detecting holiness, but also by the learned, the distinguished and the noble, both clerical and lay. This is clear from his letters, and from his conversations with the vicar-general of the Archbishop of Paris. Moreover, he was quoted several times by Fénelon (Œuvres, ii, 320, 321), whose attention had doubtless been drawn to him by the activities of this same M. de Beaufort who "tentait de prouver, contre l'évidence, que le pur amour du F. Laurent est moins excessif que celui de Fénelon."*

II

For Br. Lawrence's works we depend on two books: **Maximes spirituelles, fort utiles aux âmes pieuses pour acquérir la présence de Dieu, recueillies de quelques manuscrits du Frère Laurent de la Résurrection, religieux convers des Carmes déchaussés, avec l'abrégé de la vie de l'auteur et quelques lettres qu'il a écrites à des personnes de piété** (Paris, 1693: Bib-

---

*Histoire littéraire du sentiment religieux en France depuis la fin des guerres de religion jusqu'à nos jours. Par Henri Bremond, t. vi, pp. 392-4.

liothèque Nationale, cote D 37601) ; and Abbé de Beaufort's **Mœurs et Entretiens du Frère Laurent de la Resurrection, carme déchaussé, avec la Pratique de la Présence de Dieu, tirée de ses lettres, à Chalons, 1693** (Bibliotheque Nationale, cote 28, 27, 17.)†

In England, as in France, Br. Lawrence has endeared himself to many non-Catholic Christians. A selection of his Conversations and Letters was translated in 1724, and since then there have been some twenty different editions of selections, most, if not all, of them published under non-Catholic auspices. The present translation has been made from a reprint of the originals, excluding the **Eloge du Frère Laurent** and de Beaufort's introduction to the **Mœurs et Entretiens,** which, though full of interest and containing many sayings of Br. Lawrence, can hardly be classed among his writings.

"You will not find a merely speculative devotion set

---

†In the *Correspondence* of Bossuet, t. viii, p. 386, in a letter of October 7, 1697, there is a reference to the *Mœurs et Entretiens,* which had been adopted by Madame Guyon, and were in bad odour in consequence.

out in these pages or one which can be practiced only in the cloister. Everyone must worship and love God, and this duty cannot be properly fulfilled unless we are bound to Him by a communion of the heart which constrains us to run to Him at every moment, like little children who cannot stand upright without help from their mother. Such communion is not difficult; on the contrary, it is easy and necessary for all, and in it consists that ceaseless prayer which St. Paul imposes on all Christians. Whoever does not practise it or feel the need of it, or appreciate his own inability to do what is right, he does not know his own self nor what God is nor the continual need we all have of Jesus Christ" (M. de Beaufort).

DONALD ATTWATER

CONVERSATIONS

THE FIRST CONVERSATION

August 3, 1666

The first time that I saw Br. Lawrence he told me that Almighty God had granted him an extraordinary grace in his conversion, which had taken place at the age of eighteen, while he was still in the world. He told me—

That one winter day he noticed a tree stripped of its leaves and reflected that before long leaves would appear anew, then flowers and then the fruit, and that this consideration gave him so striking an idea of the providence and might of God that it had never since been effaced from his soul; that this idea had abstracted him altogether from the world and kindled in him so great a love for God that he was not able to say if it had at all increased during the forty odd years which had since passed.

That he had been footman to M. de Fuibert, treasurer of the Exchequer, and that he was a big clumsy fellow who smashed everything.

That he had gone into a monastery, hoping that he would be scarified for his awkwardness and for the mistakes he would make, and thus offer up his life and his happiness to God; but God had disappointed him, for he had found nothing but contentment, which made him often say to Him: "Lord, you have duped me."

That we should establish ourselves in the presence of God, talking always with Him; it was an infamous thing to leave His presence to indulge in follies.

That we should feed our souls on high thoughts of God, and so find great joy in being with Him.

That we ought to quicken our faith. It was lamentable that we had so little and that, instead of making it the rule of life, men gratified themselves with nice little devotions which they changed from day to day. The way of faith was the mind and spirit of the Church, and was able by itself to lead us to a high state of perfection.

That we ought to give ourselves entirely to God, whether in temporal or spiritual concerns, and find our happiness in doing His will, whether He lead us by the way of suffering or by the way of delight, for they are all the same to one truly resigned to Him.

That we must hold fast to faith when God tries our love by inflicting times of spiritual dryness; it is precisely then that we should make good acts of resignation to His will, for one such often advances us far upon His way.

That he was not scandalized by the wretchedness and iniquity of which he was always hearing; on the contrary, when he considered the malice of which a sinner was capable he was surprised the miseries were not greater. He prayed for sinners, but knowing that God could remedy their ills in His own time he did not grieve unduly.

That in order to give ourselves to God in the measure that He wishes of us, we must carefully watch over the impulses of our heart, which affect the actions of the soul, as well as the actions of the body; and that God would give help to this end to those who had a real desire to be united to Him.

That, if I had this desire, I was at liberty to come to him, Br. Lawrence, whenever I wished, without fear of being a nuisance: but without it I ought not to visit him again.

THE SECOND CONVERSATION

September 28, 1666

Br. Lawrence told me—

That he was always ruled by love, without any other consideration and without tormenting himself as to whether he would be lost or saved.

That he had found his resolution to make the love of God the end of all his actions the only satisfactory one. He was happy when he could pick up a straw from the ground for the love of God, seeking Him alone, nothing else, not even His gifts.

That it followed from this attitude of mind that God gave him endless grace; but in accepting the fruit of these graces—namely, the love that arose out of them—he had found it necessary to disregard their savour, since that was not God; for he knew by the Catholic faith that God was immeasurably greater than this and than anything else that he had felt. By doing thus there was brought about a wonderful struggle between God and the soul:

God giving, and the soul denying that that whicn she received was God. In this contest the soul was made so strong by faith as to be stronger than God, since He was never able to give so much that she could not deny that what He had given was Himself.

That his ecstasy and rapt were only those of a soul which toyed with such favours (instead of disregarding them entirely) and then went on to God Himself. Beyond a natural wonder, one must not be intoxicated by such things; God alone is the teacher.

That God rewarded whatever he had done for Him so quickly and so liberally that he had sometimes wished he could hide his deeds from Him so that, receiving no reward, he would have the privilege of doing something entirely for God.

That he had been very greatly troubled in mind by a belief that he would certainly be damned; all the men in the world could not have altered his conviction, but he reasoned about it in this way: "I undertook the religious life for the love of God only, and

I have tried to live only for Him; whether I am lost or saved, I want simply to go on living entirely for God; I shall have this good at least, that I shall have done all that I could to love Him until death." He had been so troubled for four years and had suffered greatly, but since then he had worried about neither Heaven nor Hell, and his life was completely free and happy. He put his sins between God and himself, to show Him how little he deserved His favours: but God none the less continued them, sometimes taking him as it were by the hand, and leading him before the whole court of Heaven, that all might see the wretch He was pleased to honour.

That perseverance is required at first in making a habit of converse with God and of referring all we do to Him, but after a little His love moves us to it without any difficulty.

That he expected a meed of grief and suffering after the consolations which God had given him, but he had not worried about it, knowing that, since he could do nothing for himself, God would not fail to give him strength to bear whatever should come.

That when there was a chance of exercising some virtue he always said to God: "'Lord, I cannot do that unless you enable me," and that then he was given the strength required, and more.

That when he was at fault he simply admitted it and said to God: "I shall never do otherwise if you leave me to myself; it is for you to prevent my falling and to correct what is wrong." He then felt assured of God's forgiveness, and did not let the failing prey on his mind.

That we ought to act very simply towards God, speaking frankly to Him, and asking His help in things as they occurred; in his experience, God never failed to give it.

That he had been sent lately into Burgundy to buy wine. This was a very hard job for him, as he was no good at business, and, furthermore, was lame in one leg, so that he could only get about the boat by sliding from cask to cask. However, he worried neither about this nor about his purchase; he told God that it was His business he was on: and he found that everything went well. He had been sent into Auvergne the previous year on a like errand; he did not know how the business had been done: but done it was, and very well done.

It was the same in the kitchen, from which he had by nature a very strong aversion: having accustomed himself to do everything there for the love of God, always praying for the grace to get through his work, he had found it quite easy all the fifteen years he had been engaged there.

That he was then in the cobbler's workshop and enjoyed it, but that he was ready to leave that job too, since he was glad to do any sort of work for the love of God.

That with him the time of prayer was not different from any other; he had set times for it, which the Father Prior had appointed, but he neither wanted nor asked for them, for the most absorbing work did not divert him from God.

That, since he knew he must love God in all things and endeavoured to do so, he had no need of a director, but a great need of his confessor to absolve him. He was very much aware of his sins, but was not discouraged by them. He confessed them to God and did not ask Him to excuse them, and when he had done so he returned in peace to his ordinary business of love and worship.

That he had not consulted anybody about his difficulties; but knowing by the light of faith that God only was present he directed all his actions towards him, come what would, and that he was willing gladly to lose all for the love of God, for that love is all-sufficing.

That our thoughts spoil everything, all the trouble begins with them. We must be careful to reject them immediately we see that they are neither necessary to our occupation at the moment nor conducive to our salvation, and return to our communion with God, wherein is our only good.

That at first his prayer had consisted entirely in rejecting distractions and falling into them again.

That he had never been able to pray according to a pattern, as some do. At first he had used vocal prayer for a time, but the practice had left him in a way he could not account for.

That he had asked to remain a novice always, as he did not believe that anyone would want to profess him, and it seemed impossible that his novitiate was over.

That he was not bold enough to ask God for mortifications, nor did he desire them. But he knew well enough that he deserved them, and that when God sent them He would also send him the grace to sustain them.

That all penitential practices and other mortifications were only useful in so far as they promoted union with God through love. He had given much thought to this, and was persuaded that the shortest way to come to God was by a continual exercise of love, doing all things for His sake.

That we ought to make a careful distinction between acts of the understanding and those of the will, for the first were of little account when compared with the second. Our business is simply to love and be happy in God.

That all possible mortifications would not serve to blot out a single sin, unless they were grounded in the love of God. We ought patiently to await the remission of our sins through the precious blood of our Lord, simply trying to love Him with all our hearts. God seemed to choose to bestow His greatest graces on those who had been the greatest sinners, for they showed forth His loving kindness even more than those who had grown up in innocence.

That he gave thought neither to death nor to his sins, neither to Heaven nor to Hell, but only to the doing of small things for the love of God—small things because he was incapable of big ones. He need trouble no further, for whatever came after would be according to God's will.

That the greatest sufferings and joys of the world could not be compared with those which he had experienced in the spiritual life, so that he feared nothing and asked nothing, except that he might not offend God.

That he had hardly any scruples, for "When I see that I am at fault I admit it and say: 'That is just like me; I can do nothing right by myself'; when I do not fail, I acknowledge that is God's doing and give thanks to Him."

THE THIRD CONVERSATION

November 22, 1666

Br. Lawrence told me—

That the foundation of his spiritual life had been a high idea and conception by faith of God: which, when he had once grasped it, he had at first only to cling to, excluding all other considerations, in order that he might do all his deeds for the love of God. When sometimes a considerable period went by without his thinking about Him, he did not disquiet himself, but acknowledged his wretchedness and returned to God with the more confidence for having experienced such sadness when he forgot Him.

That God is indeed honoured by the trust that we put in Him and fulfills it with graces.

That it was impossible, not only that God should deceive, but also that He should permit suffering for any length of time to a soul entirely given up to Him and determined to suffer all things for Him.

That he had now attained a state wherein he thought only of God. If some other thought or a temptation intruded, he felt it coming, and, such was his experience of God's prompt help, that sometimes he allowed it to approach until it was almost upon him, when he turned to God and it disappeared at once. For the same reason, when he had business to do, he did not think of it beforehand; but when it was time to do it God showed him, as in a mirror, how it should be done. For some time he had followed this plan of not anticipating difficulties; but before his experience of God's help in such matters he had been troubled when looking forward to them.

That he did not reflect upon those things which were over and done, and even scarcely adverted to that which he was actually doing, and after a meal he did not know what he had eaten. He did all, in his own simple way, for love of God, thanking Him for directing his actions and making many other "acts"; but all quite simply, in such a manner as to maintain himself in the loving presence of God.

That when outside occupation diverted his mind a little from God, some reminder from Him would seize his soul, giving it so strong a sense of God and so kindling it that he sometimes cried aloud, singing and dancing like a lunatic.

That he was more united with God during his ordinary activities than in religious exercises, in which he was generally afflicted with spiritual dryness.

That he expected before long some trouble of body or mind, and the worst would be to lose that sense of God which he had had so long; but the goodness of God assured him that He would not forsake him utterly, and would give him strength to bear whatever evil He might allow to happen to him; therefore he feared nothing and had no need to consult anybody about his spiritual state. When he had tried to do so, he had always come away more perplexed than before, and so, as he knew he was prepared to die and be lost for the love of God, he had no qualms about it. To abandon oneself entirely to God was a sure way and on it was always sufficient light whereby to go forward.

That in the beginning of the spiritual life it was necessary to act faithfully, and renounce one's own will, but after that there were joys indescribable. In times of difficulty we need only to turn to Jesus and ask for His grace, with which all things become easy.

That many souls get stuck among systems and particular devotions and neglect that love which is their real end. This can be seen at once in their works, and is the reason why we see so little solid virtue.

That neither skill nor knowledge is required to enable us to go to God, but just a heart determined to turn to Him only, to beat for Him only, and to love Him only.

THE FOURTH CONVERSATION

November 25, 1667

Brother Lawrence spoke to me, openly and with deep fervour, about his way of going to God, of which I have already related somewhat.

He told me that it consists in one good act of renunciation of all those things which we recognize do not lead to God, so that we may accustom ourselves to a continual communion with Him, a communion devoid both of vagueness and of artifice. We need only to realize that God is close to us and to turn to Him at every moment, to ask for His help to learn His will in doubtful things, and to do gladly those which we clearly perceive He requires of us, offering them to Him before we begin, and giving Him thanks when they have been finished for His honour.

That in this uninterrupted communion we are unceasingly occupied in praising, worshipping and loving God for His infinite goodness and perfection.

That we ought confidently to beseech His grace, not regarding our sins, but relying upon the infinite merits of our Lord. He had sensibly experienced that God never fails to offer His grace at our every action; but we do not perceive it when our minds have wandered from God, or if we have forgotten to ask His aid.

That in times of doubt God will always enlighten us, provided that we wish only to please Him and act for His love.

That our sanctification does not depend upon certain works, but upon doing for God that which we ordinarily do for ourselves. It was sad to see that so many people mistake the means for the end, who for reasons of human respect attach great importance to works which they do very imperfectly.

That he found the best way of reaching God was through those ordinary occupations which (so far as he was concerned) he received under obedience: doing them for the love of God and with as little regard for human respect as possible.

That it was a great delusion to imagine that prayer-time should be different from any other, for we are equally bound to be united to God by work at work-time as by prayer at prayer-time.

That his prayer was simply to realize the presence of God, at which time his soul was unconscious of aught else but love; and afterwards he found scarcely any difference, for he continued with God, praising and blessing Him with all his might. And so he passed his life in unbroken joy; yet hoping that God would give him somewhat to suffer when he should grow stronger.

That we ought once and for all to make an act of faith in God that He would not delude us, and so make a complete surrender to Him.

That we ought not to get tired of doing little things for the love of God, because He looks at the love rather than the work. And we need not be surprised at our frequent failures at first; the time will come when we shall make our acts naturally and with gladness.

That in order to submit entirely to the will of God, faith, hope and charity alone are necessary. Other considerations are unimportant and only to be used as a bridge to be passed over quickly on the way to abnegation, by confidence and love, in the Origin of all things.

That all things are possible to him who believes, less difficult to him who hopes, still less difficult to him who loves, and easiest of all to him who perseveres in all three virtues.

That the end we ought to propose to ourselves in this life is to become as good worshippers of God as we possibly can, as we hope to be His perfect worshippers for all eternity.

That when we enter upon the spiritual life we ought to consider in detail what manner of folk we are. We shall then find ourselves worthy of contempt, unworthy of the name of Christ: subject to all sorts of distress, and to numberless mischances which upset us and make us unreliable in our health, our temper

and our dispositions, whether internal or public—
in fact, people whom God must humiliate by pain
and trials both within and without. Is it then to be
wondered at that we experience crosses, temptations,
opposition, contradiction, at the hands of our fellow
men? Ought we not rather to submit to them, bear-
ing them so long as God may please, as things which
are really to our advantage? The greater the perfection to which a soul aspires, the more dependent
it is upon divine grace.

LETTERS

FROM BROTHER LAWRENCE
TO SEVERAL RELIGIOUS AND
HOLY PERSONS

FIRST LETTER

To a Nun

I take this opportunity of acquainting you with the opinions of one of our friars upon the consequences and helps that have resulted from his practice of the presence of God. Let us both profit by them.

You know that his principal aim during more than forty years "in religion" has been to be always with God and neither to do, say nor think anything which might displease Him: and this without any other object but love, the most meritorious of considerations.

He has now made such a habit of this practice that he receives divine assistance at all times and places; and for about thirty years his soul has been excited by interior joys, so continuous and so overpowering that, to prevent them being manifest outwardly, he has had to take refuge in behaviour that savours more of silliness than of sanctity.

If at times he gives way to distractions, God at once recalls him to His presence, often while he is engaged in his ordinary duties. He responds at once to these spiritual entreaties, either by a lifting-up of the heart to God, or by a loving gaze upon Him, or by such words as love may suggest: "See, my God, I am wholly yours," "Lord, make me pleasing to your heart." Thereupon it appears to him that the God of love is satisfied with these few words and again rests within his soul. Such experiences so persuade him that God may always be found in the depths of the soul that he has no doubt whatever about it in any circumstances.

You may judge by this, reverend Mother, what happiness and content is his. Having so inestimable a treasure within himself he is no longer troubled by the necessity of seeking and finding; it is always there, for him to take whenever he pleases.

He often complains of our blindness, exclaiming at our piteousness in that we are satisfied with so little. God, he says, has infinite treasure to bestow, and we are satisfied by a passing moment of devout feeling; we are blind, and our blindness stays the hand of God when He would pour out abundance of grace. But when He finds a soul imbued with a living faith He floods it with grace which, like a stream dammed up and finding a new outlet, spreads abundant waters far and wide.

Yes, indeed, we often stop these healing waters by our indifference to them. Let us check their course no longer, my dear Mother; let us go down into them, destroy the bank, and make a way for grace; let us atone for lost time; maybe we have but little longer to live; death is never far away, we die once only, let us be prepared.

Again I say, let us go into these waters ourselves; time flies by and waits not, and every man is responsible for himself. I believe that you have taken such effectual measures that you will not be taken unawares; you do well, for that is our business in life. Nevertheless we must go on working, because not to advance in the spiritual life is to go back. But those on whom the Holy Spirit has breathed go forward even when they sleep. If the vessel of our soul be still battered by winds and storms, let us wake the Lord who sleeps therein, and He will quickly calm the waves.

I have taken the liberty, my dear Mother, to express these ideas to you so that you may compare them with your own. They will serve to kindle and inspire yours if by mischance (which God forbid, for it would be indeed a misfortune) they should have cooled, be it ever so little. Let us then both recall our first enthusiasm and profit by the example and wisdom of this friar who, so little known to the world, is so well-beloved and cherished of God. I will pray for you; will you pray diligently for him who is, reverend Mother, yours in our Lord, etc.

From Paris,

June 1, 1682.

SECOND LETTER

To a Nun

I have to-day received two books and a letter from Sister N——whose profession is approaching and who, on that account, asks the prayers of your good community and your own in particular. Do not disappoint her, for she impresses on me that she has a very great confidence in them. Ask of God that she may make her sacrifice for His love alone and with a firm resolve to give herself entirely to Him. I will send you one of the books, which treats of the presence of God, wherein, in my opinion, is the whole spiritual life; it seems to me that whoever practices it properly must soon excel in virtue.

I am convinced that for the right practice of it the heart must be empty of all other things, for God wishes to possess it alone. And as He cannot occupy it alone without it is empty of all that is not Himself, so He cannot act there and do in it whatever He pleases.

There is no life in the world happier or more full of delight than one of continual communion with God—they only can realize it who have practiced and experienced it. But I do not urge you to it for that reason. We ought not to seek consolations from this practice, but to undertake it for love and because God wills it.

If I were a preacher, I would preach nothing else but the practice of the presence of God. If I were a director, I would recommend it to everybody: so necessary and even so easy do I believe it to be.

If we knew the need we have of God's grace and aid, we should not lose sight of Him even for a second. Believe me, and at once make a holy and firm resolve never again wilfully to forget Him, and to spend the rest of your days in His sacred presence, without, if He so wills, a single consolation of Heaven or of earth. Set about this work and, if you do it properly, you may be sure that you will soon see some results; I will help you with my poor prayers. I recommend myself earnestly to yours and to those of your good nuns, being theirs and, more particularly,

Yours, etc.

THIRD LETTER

To the Same

I received from Miss N——the rosaries which you gave her for me. I am surprised that you have not given me your views upon the book that I sent you, which you must have had by now. Set yourself heartily to the practice of it in your old age; it is better late than never.

I cannot understand how religious people are able to live satisfied without the practice of the presence of God. For myself, so far as I am able, I keep apart, holding Him in my soul, and while I am so with Him I fear nothing. But the least turning-away is a hell. This exercise does not wear out the body, and it is well from time to time, and even often, to deny ourselves harmless and permissible relaxations. For when a soul wants to be devoted entirely to Him, God will not suffer it to have any other delights. That is only what we should reasonably expect.

I do not mean that it is necessary to restrain oneself immoderately. No. We must serve God in a holy freedom, going about our business carefully, but without distress or anxiety, recalling the mind to God quietly and calmly whenever we find it wandering.

It is necessary, however, to put our whole trust in God, laying aside all other interests and even some of those particular devotions which, though good in themselves, we sometimes engage in ill-advisedly. They are only means to an end, and when, by this exercise of the presence of God, we are with Him who is our end, it is useless to have recourse to the means. Rather may we continue our communion of love with Him, rejoicing in His holy presence: at one time by an act of worship, of praise, of desire; at another, by an act of resignation, or of thanksgiving, or by any other means to which we may be moved.

Do not be discouraged by the distaste which you will feel on your human side; you must deal firmly with that. Often at first one thinks that it is a waste of time; but you must go on, making up your mind to persevere in it until death, whatever the difficulties may be. I recommend myself to the prayers of your community and to your own in particular.

I am, in our Lord,

Yours, etc.

From Paris,

November 3, 1685.

FOURTH LETTER

To a Woman in the World

I have great sympathy for you. If you can manage to leave the responsibility for your affairs to Mr. and Mrs. N——, and occupy yourself only with prayer, you will have done something worth doing. God does not ask much of us: a thought of Him from time to time, or an act of worship; sometimes to pray for His grace, sometimes to offer up your sufferings, sometimes to thank Him for His goodness to you, past and present; and to comfort yourself with thoughts of Him as often as you can. Lift up your heart to Him sometimes when you are at meals or in society; the least little remembrance will always be pleasing to Him. There is no need to cry very loudly, for He is nearer to us than we think.

To be with God it is not necessary to be always in church. We may make a chapel of our heart whereto we may escape from time to time to talk with Him quietly, humbly and lovingly. Everyone is capable of such close communion with God, some more, some less; He knows what we can do. Begin then; perhaps He is waiting for a single generous resolution. Have courage. There is but little time to live; you are nearly sixty-four, and I am almost eighty. Let us live and die with God; sufferings will be sweet and pleasant to us while we are with Him, and the greatest pleasures a cruel affliction without Him. May He be blessed by all. Amen.

Little by little, then, get used to worshipping Him in this way; imploring His grace, offering Him your heart sometimes during the day, very often in the course of your work if you are able to. Do not hamper yourself with set rules or forms of devotion, but go on with faith, with love and with humility. You may assure Mr. and Mrs. N——and Miss M——of my poor prayers; I am their servant and yours in our Lord.

Brother, etc.

FIFTH LETTER

To a Religious

I have not found my way of life dealt with in books, and although I am in no difficulties, I should like to have your opinion about it as a further security.

In conversation some days ago with a religious man, he told me that the spiritual life was a life of grace, which begins in a lowly fear, is increased by the hope of eternal life, and is consummated in pure love: and that each one of these states has its different stages, by which the blissful consummation is reached.

I have by no means followed these stages; on the contrary, I found from the first that they discouraged me, I know not why. It was for this reason that, when I entered religion, I resolved to give myself entirely to God in satisfaction for my sins and to renounce everything for love of Him.

During the first years my prayer was ordinarily meditation on death, judgement, Hell, Heaven, and my own sins. Thus I continued for some years, applying my mind carefully for the rest of the day, even during my work, to the presence of God, whom I knew always to be near me and often closely united with me. (This practice so heightened my notions of God that only faith was able to satisfy them.) Gradually I came to do the same thing during my set time of prayer, with great felicity and refreshment to myself. That is how I began.

I must tell you, however, that I suffered a good deal during the first ten years; the fear that I was not so devoted to God as I wished to be, the thought of my sins always before me, the unmerited goodness of God to me, all contributed to my disquiet. I kept on falling and struggling up again. It seemed to me that man, reason and God Himself were against me, and that only faith was for me. I was tortured, sometimes, by a fear of presumption, that I had claimed to achieve at once that which others attained only with difficulty: at other times, by the fancy that I was deliberately damning myself and that there was no salvation for me.

When I became resigned to live out my days amid
such adversity and dejection (which did not lessen
my trust in God, but rather increased my faith), I
suddenly found myself changed. A great inward
peace took hold of my troubled soul, my mind was
brought to a focus in a place of peace.

Since then I have walked before God in simplicity
and faith, in humility and love, trying hard to do
nothing, to say nothing, to think nothing that would
displease Him. I hope that when I have done all I can,
He will do with me according to His will. I cannot
explain to you what goes on in me now. I have no
troubles or doubts about my state, because I have no
wish but God's will, which I try to fulfill in all things;
I want not to pick up a straw from the ground except
in accordance with God's order and for sheer love of
Him.

I have given up all devotions and pieties which are
not of obligation, and instead try to keep myself
always in God's holy presence by simple attentiveness
and a loving gaze upon Him. This I may call the

actual presence of God, or to speak more accurately, an habitual, silent and hidden communion of the soul with Him. I receive such peace and spiritual joy, which sometimes manifests itself outwardly, that I often have to behave with apparent foolishness lest others should see how I am privileged.

Indeed, reverend Father, I cannot doubt that my soul has been with God for over thirty years. I have ignored many points lest I should bore you, but I think it proper to explain to you how I think of myself in relation to God, whom I conceive as my king.

I look upon myself as a leper, full of corruptions, the most wretched of men who has done all sorts of wickedness against his king. Seized by remorse, I confess all my evil deeds to Him, I implore His pardon, I cast myself into His hands that He may do what He wills with me. But this King is full of loving kindness and mercy. Instead of punishing me, He caresses me lovingly, He makes me eat at His table, He serves me with His own hands, He gives me

the keys to His treasury, He treats me as a favoured child. He talks with me, and His delight is to be with me in a thousand ways; I am forgiven and my iniquities are taken away without talking about them. The more I pray to be acceptable to His heart, the more weak and despicable I seem to myself, and the more I am beloved of God. It is thus that I look upon myself from time to time in His holy presence.

My most usual method is simple attentiveness and a loving gaze upon God, to whom I often feel united with more happiness and gratification than those of a baby at its mother's breast. Indeed, such is the inexpressible felicity I have experienced that I would willingly dare to call this state "the breasts of God."

When my thoughts are diverted, either by necessity or weakness, I am at once recalled by spiritual notions so sweet and entrancing that I do not care to speak of them. But I implore you, reverend Father, to consider my great imperfections, of which you are well aware, rather than the graces which God has showered upon my undeserving and unthankful soul.

My regular hours of prayer are a continuation of the same exercise. I then sometimes picture myself as a piece of stone, of which a mason is to make a statue; presenting myself thus before God, I ask Him to make His image perfect in my soul, and to render me entirely like to Himself. At other times I feel my whole soul and spirit uplifted without any solicitude or effort on my part; and so it remains, as it were suspended and held in God as in its centre and place of rest.

I know that some people attribute inactivity, delusion and self-love to this state. I admit there is a holy inactivity, and a happy self-love if the soul were capable of it under such conditions, because while in this state the soul is not concerned to make those acts which she has made hitherto. They were then a help; now they are a hindrance.

On the other hand, I cannot bear that this state should be called delusive, because the soul which thus enjoys God desires from it nought but Him. If I am deluded, then it is for God to remedy it that He may do as He wishes with me; I only want Him and to be His. However, you will favour me by letting me know your opinion, for which I have much respect in accordance with the esteem in which I hold yourself.

And I am, reverend Father.

Yours, etc.

SIXTH LETTER

To a Nun

Although my prayers are of little worth, you shall not be without them; I promised them to you and I shall keep my word. We should indeed be happy could we but find the treasure of which the Gospel speaks; everything else would appear worthless. Seeing that it is boundless, the more we seek, the more shall we find, so let us give ourselves up to the search without wearying, until we are successful. (He refers to several business matters and then goes on). In fact, reverend Mother, I do not know what I shall become. Peace of soul and tranquillity of spirit seem to have come to abide with me. If I were capable of suffering there would be none for me to have, and if I were allowed I would gladly submit to those of Purgatory, where I look forward to suffer in satisfaction for my sins. I only know that God protects me and that I am so tranquil that I fear nothing. What is there to fear when I am with Him? I cling to Him as much as I am able. May He be blessed by all.

Yours, etc.

SEVENTH LETTER

To a Woman in the World

We have a God of infinite goodness who knows what we need. I always thought that He would permit great affliction to you. He will come in His own time and when you least expect Him. Hope in Him more than ever; thank Him with me for the kindnesses He does you, particularly for the fortitude and patience which He gives you in your trials. That is a sure sign of His care for you; thank Him, then, and take comfort in Him.

I admire, too, the strength and pluck of Mr. N——. God has given him a good disposition and a good will, but he is still a little worldly and very youthful. I hope that the trial God has sent him will prove a wholesome medicine, and make him enter into himself. It is a chance to induce him to put his whole trust in Him who is with him everywhere; he should think upon Him as often as he can, especially in the greatest dangers.

A little lifting-up of the heart is enough; a short remembrance of God, an interior act of worship, made in haste and sword in hand, are prayers which, short as they may be, are nevertheless most pleasing to God; and far from lessening a soldier's courage in moments of danger, they increase it. Let him then think of God as much as he can: let him accustom himself little by little to this brief but salutary exercise; nobody notices it, and nothing is easier than to repeat short acts of worship often during the day. Recommend him, if you please, to think of God as often as he can in the way I have explained: it is a most fitting and necessary observance for a soldier, daily in danger of his life, and even of his salvation. I pray that God will watch over him and all his family, whom I greet, being their and your very humble, etc.

October 12, 1688.

EIGHTH LETTER

To a Nun

You tell me nothing new: you are not the only person troubled by distractions. The mind is given to roving, but the will is mistress of all our faculties, and must recall it and redirect it to its last end in God.

When the mind is untrained and has got into bad habits of wandering and dissipation, they are most difficult to overcome, and frequently draw us, against our wills, to the things of earth. I believe that one remedy is to confess our faults, humbling ourselves before God. I advise you to avoid much talking in prayer; long speeches often induce distractions. Hold yourself in prayer before God like a dumb or paralysed beggar at a rich man's gate; rivet your attention on keeping your mind in the presence of the Lord. If it wanders away from Him, don't get upset; to worry about it serves rather to distraction than to recollection: let the will bring back the mind quietly. If you persevere in this way, God will have pity on you.

One way of becoming recollected easily at the time of prayer, and of remaining so, is to keep the mind under control at other times—that is, keep it strictly in the presence of God. Being accustomed to think of Him often, it will then be more easy to remain undisturbed in prayer, or at any rate to recover from distractions. I have spoken fully in my other letters of the benefits to be found in this practice of the presence of God. Let us apply ourselves to it wholeheartedly, and pray for one another; I recommend myself also to the prayers of Sister N——, and of the reverend Mother M——, and am, in our Lord, your humble, etc.

NINTH LETTER

To the Same

I enclose a reply to the letter I have received from our
good Sister N——; have the kindness to give it to
her. She seems to me full of good will, but she wants
to go faster than grace. One cannot become holy all
at once. I recommend her to you; we ought to help
one another with advice, and still more by good example. Be so good as to tell me news of her from time
to time, and whether she is very ardent and very sub-
missive.

Let us remind ourselves often, my dear Mother, that
our only concern in this life is to please God, and that
everything else is only a vain waste of time. You and
I have lived more than forty years in religion. Have
we used them to love and serve God, who, in His
mercy, has called us to our state for that end? I am
ashamed and disgusted when I reflect, on the one
hand, upon the great graces which God has granted,
and still grants me; and, on the other, upon the ill-use

I have made of them and upon my poor progress in the way of perfection.

Since by His mercy He gives us still a little time, let us begin in earnest, let us make up for lost time, let us again turn with complete trust to that Father of mercies who is always ready to receive us affectionately. For love of Him, my dear Mother, let us give up, let us whole-heartedly give up, all that is not of Him. His due is infinitely more. Let us think upon Him without intermission. Let us put our whole confidence in Him. Without doubt we shall soon feel the effects of so doing, and shall receive a plentifulness of that grace without which we can do nothing but sin.

We cannot avoid the perils and snares of which life is full without the actual and unceasing help of God; we must then pray for it unremittingly. How can we pray to Him unless we are with Him? How can we be with Him unless we are often thinking of Him? And how can we think of Him often unless we make a holy habit of so doing? You will tell me that I keep on saying the same thing. It is true. I do not know any better or easier way; and as I follow no other myself I recommend it to everybody. We must know before we can love; and to know God we must often think about Him. And when we love Him, we shall think about Him all the more, "for where thy treasure is, there is thy heart also." Just consider it carefully.

Your very humble, etc.

March 28, 1689.

TENTH LETTER

To a Woman in the World

I have had a good deal of difficulty in making up my mind to write to Mr. N——, and I only do it now because it is the wish of yourself and Mrs. N——. Be so good, then, as to address the letter and send it to him. I am well pleased with the trust you have in God; may He ever increase it, for we cannot put too much of it in so good and faithful a friend, who will never fail us either in this world or the next.

If Mr. N—— can turn his recent loss to his own advantage and trust completely in God, He will soon give him another friend, and one more powerful and better disposed. God deals with hearts as He pleases. Perhaps Mr. N—— was attached to him whom he has lost in too worldly and inordinate a way. We ought, indeed, to love our friends, but without prejudice to the love of God, which comes first.

Do remember what I have advised you: that is, to think often of God, by day, by night, whatever you are doing, in your duties, even in your amusements. He is always near you and with you; do not neglect Him. You would think it rude to leave a friend, who came to visit you, alone; why then leave God alone? Do not then forget Him, think about Him often—to do so is the proper business of a Christian: if we do not know our calling we must learn it. I will help you with my prayers.

I am, in our Lord, yours, etc.

From Paris,

October 29, 1689.

ELEVENTH LETTER

To a Nun

I do not pray that you may be delivered from your sufferings, but I ask God earnestly to give you strength and patience to bear them so long as He pleases to afflict you. Fortify yourself with Him who fastens you to the cross; He will deliver you in His own time. Happy are those who suffer with Him. Accustom yourself to such pain, and pray for strength to endure all He wills, and for so long as He may think fit. The world does not understand these truths, nor am I surprised. Worldly people suffer after their kind, and not in a Christian way; they look on sickness as an affliction of nature, not as a gift of God, and for that reason they find in it only the hardness and rigour of nature. But those who look upon sickness as coming from the hand of God, as an evidence of His solicitude, as a means which He chooses for their salvation, commonly find great happiness and solace in it.

I wish you could realize that God is often nearer to us in time of ill-health and weakness than when we are well. Seek no other physician but Him, for to my mind He wishes to heal us Himself; put your whole trust in Him, and you will soon benefit; we often delay recovery by trusting to medicine rather than to Him. Whatever remedies you make use of they will only succeed so far as He allows; when pain comes from God, He only can cure it, and He often sends disorders of the body to cure those of the soul. Comfort yourself with the all-powerful Physician of both souls and bodies.

I can see that you will retort that I am very much at my ease, eating and drinking at the table of the Lord—and not without reason. But do you imagine it would be comfortable for the biggest blackguard in the world to eat at his king's table, and to be waited on by the royal hands, if he had no assurance of the royal pardon? I think he would feel exceedingly uneasy and that only confidence in the goodness of his sovereign could ease his mind. And so, I assure you, whatever pleasures I may experience at the table of my King, the consciousness of my sins, to say nothing of the uncertainty of their forgiveness, is exceedingly distressing — though I must admit that the distress is acceptable to me.

Be content with the state of life which God has allotted to you; however happy you may think me, I envy you. If I might suffer with God, my pains and afflictions would be Heaven; without Him, the greatest pleasures would be Hell: all my happiness would be to suffer something for His sake.

I must, in a little time, go to God—that is to say, go to Him for judgement. If I can see God for one short moment the punishments of Purgatory will be sweet, even if they last to the end of this world. My consolation now is that I see God by faith, and I see Him in such a way that I sometimes can almost say: "I believe no longer, for I can see." I experience that which we are taught by faith, and in that assurance and working of faith I will live and die with Him.

Cling to God always. He is the one and only help in your troubles, and I beseech Him to be with you. I greet Mother Prioress and ask the prayers of her, of the community and of yourself; and I am, in our Lord.

Yours, etc.

November 17, 1690.

TWELFTH LETTER

To a Nun

Since you wish so earnestly that I should communicate to you the means I have followed to reach this state of the presence of God, to which our Lord has willed that I should attain, I will give in to your importunity, but very unwillingly and only on condition that you show my letter to no one. If I thought that you would let it be seen, all my desire for your perfecting would not induce me to write it. What I can tell you about it is this:

Having found different ways of attaining to God and different practices of the spiritual life in many different books, I came to the conclusion that they would serve to hinder rather than to help me in my quest, which was for nothing else but a way of becoming wholly God's. So I made up my mind to give all to gain all, and, after giving myself up entirely to God in satisfaction for my sins, I renounced everything in the world that came between Him and me. Sometimes I looked on myself as a poor criminal before his judge; at other times I looked on Him in my heart as my Father and my God, worshipping Him as often as I was able, and recollecting myself whenever my mind was distracted from His holy presence. I found no little difficulty in this exercise, but I persevered in spite of my failures, not worrying or blaming myself when my distractions were involuntary. I did this not only at my set times of prayer, but at all times driving away from my mind everything that could displace the thought of God, every hour, every minute, even at my busiest moments.

Such, reverend Mother, has been my practice ever since I entered religion, and, though I have grievously given way to slackness and weakness, I have received very great benefits thereby. That I owe these to the mercy and goodness of God I know well enough: for we can do nothing without Him, I less than any. But by keeping ourselves faithfully in His presence and setting Him always before our eyes, not only do we hinder ourselves from displeasing Him, at any rate wilfully, but we also gain a holy liberty to ask for those graces of which we stand in need. In fact, by so often repeating these acts they become habitual, and the presence of God becomes, as it were, natural. Give Him thanks, if you please, with me for His great goodness towards me; I can never be sufficiently grateful for the numberless favours He has bestowed on so wretched a sinner. May He be praised by all. Amen.

I am, in our Lord,

Yours, etc.

THIRTEENTH LETTER

To a Nun

If our practice of the presence of God were more habitual, our bodily maladies would be alleviated. God often allows us to suffer somewhat in order to purify our souls, and so bring us nearer to Him. My own experience is such that I cannot understand how a soul that lives with God and desires only Him can be capable of misery.

Be brave! Keep on offering your sufferings to Him and pray for strength. Above all, make a habit of communing with Him, and forget Him as little as you can. Adore Him amidst your sufferings, offer yourself to Him, and when your pain is at its worst ask humbly and lovingly, as a child from her father, for resignation to His holy will and for the assistance of His grace. I will accompany you with my poor and feeble prayers.

God has many ways of drawing us to Him. Sometimes He hides Himself from us, but faith, which alone never fails us at need, should be our support and the cornerstone of our trust which must be all in God.

I don't know what God will do with me. I am always happy. Everybody else suffers while I, who ought to be visited by the severest discipline, am conscious of joys so prolonged and piercing that I have difficulty in restraining them. I would willingly ask of God a share in your sufferings, but I know that my weakness is such that, if He left me to myself for a moment, I should become the most worthless man alive. And yet I do not know how He could leave me alone, since faith has brought me so close to Him and He never goes away from us unless we desert Him first. Let us fear to separate ourselves from Him; let us be always with Him, living and dying in His presence. Pray for me, as I will for you.

Yours, etc.

November 28, 1690.

FOURTEENTH LETTER

To the Same

I am grieved that you suffer for so long, but my pity is leavened by the certainty that your suffering is a proof of God's love for you: look on it as such and you will find it easier to bear. My own opinion is that you should give up all human remedies and resign yourself entirely to divine providence; God may be only waiting for such a mark of your trust to cure you. There would be no question of "tempting providence" seeing that, so far from having any good effect, these remedies have made you worse.

I said in my last letter that God sometimes allows the body to suffer for the good of the soul. Take courage, then; make a virtue of necessity; ask God, not to take away your physical ills, but for strength to bear them bravely for His sake, and for so long as may please Him. Truly such a prayer is difficult to our human nature, but it is very pleasing to God and sweet to those that love Him. Love eases pain, and when one loves God one suffers for Him with gladness and courage. Do this, I beseech you: comfort yourself with Him who is the only cure for all our ills, who is the Father of the afflicted, who is always ready to help us and who loves us immeasurably more than we imagine. Love Him and cease to seek relief elsewhere: I hope you will soon receive it. Farewell. I will assist you with my prayers, poor as they are, and shall be always in our Lord.

Yours, etc.

This morning, being the feast of St. Thomas, I have offered holy communion for your intention.

FIFTEENTH LETTER

To the Same

Thank God that you have been somewhat eased, according to your wish. I have been nearly dead several times and have never been so content as then; accordingly, I asked for no relief, but only for strength to submit bravely, humbly and lovingly. Be brave, my dear Mother, for it is good to suffer with God: however grievous your burdens, take them up with love. It is blissful to suffer in His company, and, if we want to taste of Heaven in this world, we must cultivate a close and humble and loving communion with Him; we must keep our minds from wandering away at any time; we must make our hearts a sanctuary where He is always worshipped; we must watch vigilantly lest we do or say or think anything displeasing to Him. Suffering will be a happiness, a balm and a consolation while we are thus occupied with God.

I know that in arriving at this state the beginning is very difficult, for we must walk entirely by faith.

But we know we can do all things with the grace of God, and that He never withholds from those who entreat Him earnestly. Knock at the door, keep on knocking, and I tell you that, if you are not discouraged, He will open it in due time and give all of a sudden what He has withheld for so long. Farewell. Pray to Him for me as I do for you; I hope to see Him soon.

I am yours, in our Lord, etc.

January 22, 1691.

SIXTEENTH LETTER

To the Same

God knows well enough what we need, and that all that He does is for our good. If we realized how much He loves us we should be ready to receive from Him either the sweet or the bitter with indifference; the hardest and most disagreeable trials would be welcome. The sorest afflictions are a burden only because of the way we look at them; when we really believe that the God whose hand chastens us with humiliation, grief and pain, is actually a most loving Father, the bitterness of His visitations disappears and we rejoice in them.

We must concentrate on knowing God: the more we know Him, the more we want to know Him. And, as knowledge is commonly the measure of love, the deeper and wider our knowledge, the greater will be our love. And if our love of God is great, we shall love Him equally in sorrow and in joy.

We must not hinder ourselves by looking for, or loving God because of, any perceptible favours, however sublime, which He has done or may do for us; such graces, great as they may be, do not bring us so near to Him as does one simple act of faith. Let us seek Him by faith; He is in the midst of us, and we do not need to look for Him elsewhere. Is it not disrespectful, and even blameworthy, to leave Him while we amuse ourselves with trifling matters which do not please Him and may even be offensive to Him? He tolerates them, but I fear that one day these trivialities will cost us dear.

We must devote ourselves to Him in good earnest, casting everything else out of our hearts; He wishes to be alone therein, so let us pray for that grace. If we do our best on our side, we shall soon see in ourselves the alteration that we hope for.

I cannot thank Him enough for the relief He has given you. I hope from His mercy the happiness of seeing Him within a few days. *Let us pray for one another. I am, in our Lord,

Yours, etc.

February 6, 1691.

*He died within the week—Tr.

SPIRITUAL
MAXIMS

ON FAITH

All things are possible to him who believes, less difficult to him who hopes, still less difficult to him who loves, and easiest of all to him who perseveres in all three virtues. All those who are baptized and hold the faith have taken the first step on the road to perfection, and may become perfect to the extent that they persevere according to the following counsel.

1. We should refer to God and His glory all that we do and say and undertake, setting before ourselves the task of becoming true worshippers of Him in this world, as we hope to be His perfect worshippers in the world to come; and making a strong resolution to overcome by His grace all the difficulties which beset us in the spiritual life.

2. We must believe steadfastly that such difficulties are for our own good; that it is God's will that we should be afflicted; that it is according to divine providence that we should be subject to all kinds of

conditions, to suffer all kinds of chastening, of woe and of temptation, for the love of God and for so long as He pleases: there can be no true devotion and perfection without such submission of the heart and mind to the will of God.

3. The greater the perfection to which a soul aspires, the more dependent is she upon divine grace, and this grace becomes more necessary every moment because without it the soul can do nothing. The world, the flesh and the Devil together wage so fierce and unremitting a war that, without actual grace and a humble reliance thereon, the soul would be dragged down in spite of herself. Such dependence seems hard to human nature, but grace makes it acceptable and a refuge.

NECESSARY PRACTICES FOR ATTAINING THE SPIRITUAL LIFE

1. The most holy, the most general and the most necessary practice in the spiritual life is the practice of the presence of God, whereby the soul finds her joy and contentment in His companionship, talk-

ing humbly and lovingly to Him always and at all times, without rule or system, but particularly in moments of temptation, of trouble, of spiritual dryness, of revulsion, and especially when we fall into unfaithfulness and sin.

2. We should try unceasingly to allow each one of our actions to become a moment of communion with God: not a studied act, but just as it comes from purity and simplicity of heart.

3. We must act recollectedly, not with that impetuosity and thoughtlessness that mark an undisciplined mind; and we must work quietly, calmly and lovingly before God, beseeching Him to accept our labours. By such unceasing turning to God we shall crush the head of Satan and strike his weapons from his hands.

4. During our work and other activities, during our spiritual reading or study, yes, even in our set devotions and vocal prayer, we ought to stop for a moment, as often as we can, in order to worship God in our hearts, to touch Him as it were by stealth

as He passes. Since you know that God is with you in all your actions, that He is at the very depth and centre of your soul, why not then pause an instant in your external occupations, and even in your prayers, to worship Him inwardly, to praise Him, to petition Him, to offer Him your heart and to thank Him?

What can be more pleasing to God than this quitting many times a day of material things, in order to withdraw within ourselves and worship Him? Furthermore, these moments of recollection little by little purge us of those things of sense, among which alone self-love can flourish.

Indeed, we can give God no more convincing evidence of our faithfulness than often to put aside and avoid the creature, that we may rejoice for one moment in the Creator.

I am not proposing to you to give up material things entirely; that is impossible. Prudence, the queen of virtues, must be your guide. Nevertheless, I maintain that it is a common mistake among religious people to neglect this periodical recollection in which they may worship God inwardly and enjoy for a few moments the peace of His holy presence. The digression has been long, but no longer than I believe the matter to require; let us then return to our subject.

5. All these acts of worship must be the fruit of faith. We must believe that God is indeed within our hearts, and that we must worship, love and serve Him in spirit and in truth; that He knows all that happens or can happen among His creatures; that He is self-existent, while we depend entirely upon Him; that His infinite perfections are of such sovereign excellence and authority that we are required to put everything, ourselves, our souls and bodies at the disposition of His will now and for ever; that in justice we owe Him our thoughts, our words and our deeds. Let us see that we act accordingly.

6. We must diligently examine our conscience to find out of what virtues we are most in need, and which are the most difficult for us to acquire; and to learn

our habitual sins and the occasions upon which we generally fall into them. In times of temptation we should go straight to God with complete trust; remain recollected in His presence, humbly worshipping the divine majesty: tell Him our woes and weaknesses: lovingly beg for the aid of His grace; and we shall find in Him the strength that we ourselves lack.

HOW WE MUST WORSHIP GOD IN SPIRIT AND TRUTH

There are three points to be answered in this question:

1. To worship God in spirit and in truth means to render to Him that worship which is His due; God is a spirit—therefore He must be worshipped in spirit and in truth, by a lowly and genuine worship in the depth of our soul which God alone can see. It is possible to give Him this worship so often that it becomes almost natural, as though God were one with our soul and our soul one with God. Practice only will explain this.

2. To worship God in truth is to acknowledge Him to be what He is, and ourselves to be what we are. To worship God in truth is to recognize clearly, certainly, and with all our faculties, that God is that which He is, infinitely perfect, immeasurably removed from evil, and therefore full of all divine attributes. Is not the man unreasonable who does not use all his powers in reverence for, and worship of, this mighty God?

3. To worship God in truth is to admit that we separate ourselves from Him, although He would make us like to Himself if only we wished it. Is it not foolish to withhold from Him, even for a minute, the reverence, the love, the service and the ceaseless worship that we owe Him?

OF THE UNION OF THE SOUL WITH GOD

There are three kinds of union—the habitual, the virtual and the actual.

1. Habitual union is when one is united to God simply by grace.

2. Virtual union is when one begins an action whereby one is united to God, and remains with Him by virtue of that action for such time as it continues.

3. Actual union is the most complete, and, being entirely supernatural, the most powerful: for the soul is not passive as in the other two states. Rather is she intensely active, her movements kindling more warmth tnan does fire and creating more light than does the clear sun. Yet our feelings can deceive us as to this union, for it is not merely an emotion, as when our hearts urge us to exclaim: "My God, I love you with my whole being," or such-like words. It is rather an indefinable something of the soul, beauteous, peaceful, unearthly, reverent, humble, loving and very simple: it lifts the soul up to God, impelling her to love Him, to worship Him, even to embrace Him with caresses which cannot be expressed and which only experience can make us understand.

4. All who aim at union with God should know that

whatever can divert the will towards Him is also welcome and pleasing to it: the will makes it so.

Everybody must admit that the ways of God are past our understanding, and, therefore, to become united to Him the will must be deprived of all its tastes and pleasures, spiritual and material. Then, being thus stripped, it is free to love God above all things; for if the will is able in any degree to know God, it can only be through love. There is a great difference between the tastes and fancies of the will and the workings of the same will; for its preferences and conceits are within the soul as in their bounds, but its operation, which is love, has its end in God.

ON THE PRESENCE OF GOD

1. The presence of God is an applying of our spirit to Him, or a realization of His presence which can be brought about either by the imagination or the understanding.

2. I know one who, for forty years, has practised the presence of God intellectually, and he gives it

several other names. Sometimes he calls it a simple act, or a clear and distinct knowledge of God: sometimes an impression or a loving gaze or a sense of God; yet other times he calls it a waiting on God, a silent conversation with Him, a divine repose, the life and peace of the soul. He says, however, that all these expressions for the presence of God are synonyms, they express the same thing, that presence which has come to be natural to him, in this way:

3. By repeated acts and by frequently recalling his mind to God he has developed such a habit that, as soon as he is free from external occupations, and even often while he is still busy, his very soul, without any forethought on his part, is lifted above all earthly things, maintained and as it were upheld in God, as in its consummation and place of rest. At such times faith is nearly always with him, and his spirit is satisfied. It is this which he calls the actual presence of God, which includes all other kinds and much more besides, so that he lives now as if there were only God and himself in the world: conversing

always with Him, entreating Him at need, and rejoicing with Him in a thousand ways.

4. Now it should be observed that this communion
with God is held in the depth of the soul, at its very
centre: it is there that the soul speaks heart to heart
with God amid a wonderful peace wherein the spirit
experiences the keenest joy. All that goes on outside
is no more to the soul than as a fire of straw which,
the more it flares, the sooner it is burnt out, and
rarely and little do exterior concerns disturb the interior peace.

5. But to return to our own consideration of the subject, I tell you that the lovingness of God insensibly
kindles so burning a flame of love in the soul that
embraces Him, that one has to moderate its outward
expression.

6. We should be surprised if we knew what converse
the soul sometimes holds with God, who seems so
much to delight in such communion that He allows
anything to the soul which desires to rest in Him
and in His heart. And, as if He feared lest she should

return to the things of earth, He is careful to provide for her all she could possibly desire, so that she finds within herself a feast of heavenly delights, though she herself has done nothing towards it, and brings to it only her happiness.

7. The presence of God is then the life and nourishment of the soul, which, by God's grace, may attain it by the following means.

MEANS FOR ATTAINING THE PRESENCE OF GOD

1. The first means is a great purity of life.

2. The second is a great faithfulness in the practice of His presence, and in keeping the soul's gaze upon God, quietly, humbly and lovingly, without giving way to difficulties or worries.

3. Take care that you begin your actions, continue them, and finish them with an inward lifting of the heart to God. And as it takes time and trouble to acquire this habit, so you need not be discouraged by failure; as its formation is difficult, so will your joy be great when it is attained.

Is it not right that the heart, which is the seat of life governing the rest of the body, should be the first and last to love and worship God, both in beginning and finishing our works, spiritual and temporal, and generally throughout the business of life? It is the heart, therefore, that must ensure this turning to God, which, as I have already said, can more easily be done spontaneously and without study.

4. It is helpful for those who undertake this practice to use interiorly short ejaculations, such as: "My God, I am wholly yours"; "O God of love, I love you with all my heart"; "Lord, make my heart like yours"; or any other such words as love may suggest at the moment. But care must be taken that the mind does not wander and return again to the world; keep it turned to God only, so that, controlled and subdued by the will, it cannot but rest in God.

5. This practice of the presence of God is not easy at the outset, but if persevered in it produces imperceptibly wonderful works in the soul; it draws down from the Lord an abundance of grace and leads

insensibly to that simple gaze of love, to that sight of God's continual presence, which is the most simple, and the most fruitful kind of prayer.

6. Notice, if you please, that to attain this state the control of the senses is taken for granted. It is impossible for a soul inordinately fond of earthly things to find complete joy in the presence of God, for to be with the Creator it is necessary wholly to give up whatever is created.

THE BENEFITS OF THE PRESENCE OF GOD

1. The first benefit which the soul receives from the presence of God is that faith becomes more alive and active on every side of life, particularly in times of need, since it obtains for us grace in temptation and in our dealings with one another. For the soul, accustomed by this practice to rely on faith, seeing and feeling God present, is able to call upon Him freely and with confidence, and to obtain that of which she is in need. One may say that faith enables the soul to approach the state of the Blessed; the more she

advances the more living does faith become, and at last it becomes so quickened that the soul can almost say: "I no longer believe, for I can see and experience."

2. The practice of the presence of God strengthens us in hope. Our hope grows in proportion as our knowledge, and as our faith is enabled by this holy practice to penetrate the mysteries of God, in that measure it finds in Him a beauty which infinitely surpasses not only that of the bodies which we behold on earth, but also that of perfected souls and of the angels. Our hope then increases and strengthens, encouraged and sustained by the magnitude of the good which it desires to enjoy, and which, in some sort, it already savours.

3. Hope imbues the will with a contempt for the world and inflames it with the fire of divine love. God's love is a consuming fire which burns to ashes whatever is contrary to it, and the soul thus kindled can live only in the presence of God, that presence which inspires within the heart a holy ardour, a

sanctified eagerness, a veritable passion to see God loved, known, served and worshipped by all His creatures.

4. By this practice the soul comes to such a knowledge of God that almost all her life is passed in making acts of love and of worship, of contrition and of trust, of thanks, of offering, of petition, and of all virtues; sometimes, indeed, she seems engaged in one unceasing, endless act, for the soul is keeping herself continually in the divine presence.

I know that only a few persons attain this state; it is a grace which God bestows on certain chosen souls, for this "simple regard" is an uncovenanted gift. But for the encouragement of those who wish to undertake this holy practice, I must say that He ordinarily gives it to those who are properly disposed; and if He does not give it, one can, with the assistance of ordinary grace and by the practice of the presence of God, acquire at least a way and state of prayer which approaches very nearly to that of "simple regard."